DROPPIN' KNOWLEDGE ON FOUNDATIONAL SKILLS

DROPPIN'
KNOWLEDGE ON
FOUNDATIONAL
SKILLS

Heidi Martin

Adam Martin

DROPPIN' KNOWLEDGE ON FOUNDATIONAL SKILLS

Phonological and Phonemic Awareness Exercises Aligned to the Science of Reading

JB JOSSEY-BASS™

A Wiley Brand

Contents

Contents

About the Authors

Heidi Martin is trained in LETRS for Early Childhood, IMSE Orton-Gillingham, and Top 10 Tools. She is a National Facilitator for LETRS EC. She has presented at national conferences as well as provided training at the district level. Heidi is the author of *P is for Paint*, which is the one and only alphabet book with embedded mnemonics. She has authored and self-published the *Decodable Adventure* Series books. She taught first grade for over 10 years and most recently taught Kindergarten and 4K.

Adam Martin is a National LETRS Facilitator certified for Units 1–8 and presents to teachers and districts on a weekly basis. He has his Masters in Educational Literacy and his Reading Specialist License. He is the co-author and editor for the *Decodable Adventure* Series books. He taught first grade for seven years and has tutored children of all ages.

How to Contact the Authors

We appreciate your input and questions about this book! Email us at hello@droppinknowledge.com or visit our website at www.droppinknowledge.com.

Other Books in the *Droppin' Knowledge* Series

Droppin' Knowledge on Sight Words and Word Mapping: High-Frequency Word Activities Aligned to the Science of Reading

Droppin' Knowledge on Phonics: Spelling and Phonics Activities Aligned to the Science of Reading

Hey, Parents and Teachers!

We are so excited to help you teach reading! We are Heidi and Adam Martin—both former first-grade teachers (and parents) who now spend our time sharing the Science of Reading with as many people as we can! But before this, we **had no idea there was a science to how we learn to read**. We taught first grade for a combined 15+ years using what most people call "balanced literacy" methods until we found that there is actual science to how we learn to read.

We also learned that according to the 2022 Nation's Report Card, less than 40% of kids are reading proficiently.[1] To us, this was a big wake-up call. If over 60% of our kids are not reading proficiently, we must be doing something wrong!

Once we learned there was decades of evidence and research on how we learn to read, we set out on a mission to unlearn and learn it all. We want to let you know that this has been a journey, not a sprint. There was a lot for us to unlearn (and still is). Throughout this journey of unlearning, we definitely had to work through some ups and downs, as well as emotions of frustration, anger, and regret. The fact that we were not taught this earlier, especially since this science has been around for over 20 years, can really weigh on you. We often think back to the kids we could have helped if we only knew what we know now. However, you don't know better until you do, so we just have to move forward and make sure this doesn't happen again. If some of this is new to you as well, please remember to give yourself grace!

Let's talk about some of the terms we have been using and clarify where we came from and where we are now.

What Is Balanced Literacy?

Balanced literacy sounds good, doesn't it? I mean who doesn't love being balanced? Heidi was sold on this, especially being a type B teacher. She was not a fan of words like "systematic" and "structured." Then, she found out that balanced literacy is not truly balanced after all. Adam was starting his teaching career while being taught about the Science of Reading through his licensure program. However, in our school district, we were using balanced literacy curriculums. Going through hours of professional development on this curriculum, this became the norm. Since this was all the buzz, it had to be the most beneficial thing for our

---

[1]https://www.nationsreportcard.gov/reading/nation/achievement/?grade=4.

students, right? Adam said, "I had my skepticisms on balanced literacy, especially since I was seeing minimal progress from my students. I think this is the case for a lot of teachers."

To be clear, when we say balanced literacy, we are talking about programs and strategies that were most often used in schools and called "balanced" within those schools and programs. In reality, these programs skip many of the foundational reading skills kids need in order to become successful readers.

Balanced literacy was supposed to be the answer to the reading wars—a compromise. However, in our experience, there is much more of the whole language approach in balanced literacy programs. We feel that these "balanced literacy" programs are not truly balanced after all. Some examples of the remnants of whole language are:

- Skipping a word if you don't know it

- Using meaning or context to solve or read a word

- Believing that reading is natural (aka reading more will help kids become good readers)

- Memorizing "sight words" or spelling words

If our kids cannot decode and read the words on a page (or if they are skipping words), how will they "naturally" become skilled readers? We have learned from the research on how we learn to read that the continuum, or progression of learning to read, is NEVER truly balanced. We spend more time on specific skills when students are developing foundational reading skills than we do later on once those skills and abilities to decode are mastered. The time spent on specific skills will vary based on where our kids are in their reading development. So, although it sounds good, there is never really a "balance" to literacy.

What Is the Science of Reading?

You have probably heard the term "Science of Reading" more times than you can count, but the definition can get a little muddy. So let's talk about what the Science of Reading is **not**.

The Science of Reading is not a curriculum.

The Science of Reading is not just phonics.

The Science of Reading is not a strategy or activity.

Here is how The Reading League defines the Science of Reading[2]:

The Science of Reading is a vast, interdisciplinary body of scientifically based research about reading and issues related to reading and writing. This research has been conducted over the last five decades across the world.

It is derived from thousands of studies conducted in multiple languages. The Science of Reading has culminated in a preponderance of evidence to inform how proficient reading and writing develop, why some have difficulty, and how we can most effectively assess and teach and, therefore, improve student outcomes through prevention of and intervention for reading difficulties.

The Science of Reading is derived from researchers from multiple fields:

Cognitive psychology

Communication sciences

Developmental psychology

Education

Implementation science

Linguistics

Neuroscience

School psychology

To break that down, we like to say that **the Science of Reading is the research and the evidence on how our brains learn to read**. This means that not just one study is referenced when discussing the skills kids need to read. Again, this is

---

[2]https://www.thereadingleague.org/wp-content/uploads/2022/03/Science-of-Reading-eBook-2022.pdf.

research that has been conducted for almost 50 years and includes research of the research (meta-analysis)!

We hope that helps explain some of the terms you may have been hearing about and why we decided to write these books. We are so excited for you to use these activities with your students and/or your own children. The activities in this book will help you ensure your students have the foundational skills they need to become successful readers. These skills are often what is missing for older students who are struggling to read.

To this day, we think of all of our kids who were struggling to read that we probably could have helped if we had only known about these skills. Their names, their faces, and their struggles replay in our heads on a regular basis. We often have to remind ourselves that **we don't know better until we do**. Although the guilt still creeps up from time to time, we try to focus on what we can control. Now that we know how important these skills are, we can help others teaching kids to read by sharing what we have learned.

By giving kids these **oh-so-important foundational skills**, we are setting them up for reading success!

Our main goal with this book is to give teachers and parents an introduction to the skills that are necessary for reading success. These methods are based on over 40 years of research on the Science of Reading (SoR) and have been shown to be the greatest predictors of future reading success.

Unfortunately, as we discussed earlier, many of us were not aware of the science that exists. We have spent countless hours researching what the science says and internalizing it to be able to share it in a way that makes sense for everyone. We want to make this as easy as possible for you!

We started phonological awareness with our son when he was 3 (almost 4). He went to preschool, able to read books. Our goal was not to get him to read faster. We just wanted to make sure we gave him the foundation he needed to be successful. The magical (or should we say, scientific) thing is that now reading seems to come easy for him since he has phonological and phonemic awareness. Every child is different and while this may not be your experience, we can tell you that these skills are essential and do not always come naturally to many students. Taking the time to explicitly teach these skills is important for all learners!

Oral Language Development

One of the first foundational "bedrock" skills we want to discuss is oral language. From the vast amount of research on how our brains learn to read, we have been taught that reading does NOT come naturally to us as humans. The process of being able to read first comes from the development of speech. We are naturally programmed to learn speech, or oral language, and this in turn gives us a foundation to begin to learn how to read. We like to say in the literacy world that we go from *speech* to *print*.

So what does that mean for us as teachers and parents of young children?

We want to really help set the stage for our kids by talking to them and reading aloud to them from birth and well into their schooling. When we say "talk" to them, we want to make them a part of our world and include them in as many and all conversations we are having as possible. What this is doing is helping expose them to our language, syntax, or the order in which words work to form sentences, vocabulary (semantics), background knowledge, and pragmatics (how we use words in a professional or a personal manner). We should be talking to our kids!

More importantly when we are talking to our kids, we should have breaks and allow them to join in on the conversation. The term for this is called conversational turns. A conversational turn is the back-and-forth dialogue between an adult and a child. This can be a smile, acknowledgment, gesture, coo from a baby, or any verbal input from the child within five seconds of the adult's speech. This works the other way as well, if a child says something, or if a baby coos, and the adult responds back to the child in under five seconds, you are creating a conversational turn.

LENA (Language Environment Analysis) is a nonprofit that conducted many studies, with tens of thousands of hours of recorded conversations, and provided evidence that **conversational turns are one of the biggest predictive measures of children's reading success**, more than just having them listen to adult speech alone.[3]

---

[3]LENA. 2020. Inside Early Talk: Our point of greatest leverage for improving children's futures. Retrieved from https://www.lena.org/inside-early-talk-improving-childrens-futures/.

So we want to make sure we are speaking to our kids, and having them participate within those conversations. It is recommended to have about 40 conversational turns within an hour. This may seem like a lot, but you can easily get 10 conversational turns in under a minute if you are just discussing something while a child is playing.

When we are talking and conversing with our kids, we want to include higher-level vocabulary and multisyllabic words. We know and have done it ourselves, that when we speak to our kids we sometimes lower our vocabulary. However, we should use higher-level language. This is to help expose our kids to the expansiveness of our language. We are not expecting our kids to be able to read or spell those words right away, but through this exposure, we are adding these words to their oral language vocabulary.

We want our kids to hear those words and also use them, so again, we should help them understand and talk with them about those words. This will enable them to begin to use those words as well. To help them understand bigger, multisyllabic words, we can compare them to words that they might know that mean the same thing (synonyms). We can also talk about opposite-meaning words (antonyms), and add new/interesting words to everyday routines.

For example, instead of saying "Can you clean up your mess?", you can say, "Could you organize and sanitize your messy area?" Also, when we use a specific word, we can categorize that word. We can discuss with our kids if it is a word from nature, a word that has to do with transportation, a word that has to do with weather, etc. A benefit of this, especially if you start this from an early age with your child, is when they get to school and are reading and they come across a word they have not decoded yet, they will have a higher rate of success decoding and/or spelling that word if they know the meaning and/or have heard that word before. This benefits vocabulary development as well, because if a child has a high number of words they know the meanings to, when they enter school, it is easier for their brain to learn and categorize a higher amount of new words because of that background knowledge.

Another way to help build our kids' oral language development is through read-alouds. Reading books to our kids is a fun and engaging way to help them to learn about our world through stories. This is also a way to build their vocabulary through the rich and expansive words that authors use in text. When we read to our kids, we can even include them in the fun and get in those conversational turns by having them engage and interact with what we are reading. If the book says "They bent down and touched their toes," have the kids bend and touch their toes. Ask questions and have kids make predictions as you are reading through the story. Make connections to the feelings and actions of the characters.

All of this allows kids to understand and make connections to how the words work in the structure of those sentences, develop new understandings from the vocabulary, and provide background knowledge to how the world around them is working. You should read as often as possible as well as explore a variety of different topics and genres. With so many books being written as we speak, we have access to all types of topics and books that our kids can learn from and even relate to. Books are a great resource to develop oral language, vocabulary, background knowledge, and also pragmatics.

Oral language development starts when kids are born and can be the first crucial area to establish the basis of language our kids need before they begin to learn how to read.

Phonological and Phonemic Awareness

Next, let's talk about the crucial building blocks that will lay the foundation for our students to read. This is phonological and phonemic awareness. First, we want to explain what phonological and phonemic awareness actually means because if they are this important, we need to make sure we really understand it!

What Are Phonological Awareness and Phonemic Awareness?

Phonological awareness is a continuum of skills that kids develop with oral language. So, it is the child hearing the words, patterns, and sounds in our language, and being able to play with (or manipulate) those words, patterns, and sounds.

Phonemic awareness is part of the phonological awareness continuum. Let's break this down even further. When we talk about phonological awareness skills, we typically talk about the following skills:

Words and sentences (can the kids hear and count how many words are in a sentence)

Rhyming (words with the same middle and ending sound like mat and hat)

Syllables (parts of a word revolving around a vowel; e.g. Oc-to-pus has three syllables)

Onset (within a syllable, this is the part before the vowel sound; e.g. the -b in "bat" or the -sn in "snack." Please note that there does not have to be an onset in each syllable, like the word "if" does not have an onset because there is nothing before the vowel.)

Rime (within a syllable, this is the vowel and everything after it; e.g. the -at in "bat" and the -ack in "snack")

These are the bigger units of language. The goal of teaching these skills is to get to phonemic awareness.

Phonemic awareness refers to individual sounds in words. So these are the smaller units of language. When we talk about phonemic awareness, we are talking about isolating sounds, blending sounds into words, segmenting words into sounds, adding and deleting sounds in words, substituting sounds in words, and reversals.

> **A little trick that helped us remember the difference between phonological and phonemic awareness is to think about the actual size of those words. The word *phonological* is a longer word. It is a bigger word, which refers to the bigger units of language. *Phonemic* is a smaller word, which refers to the smaller sounds in our language.**

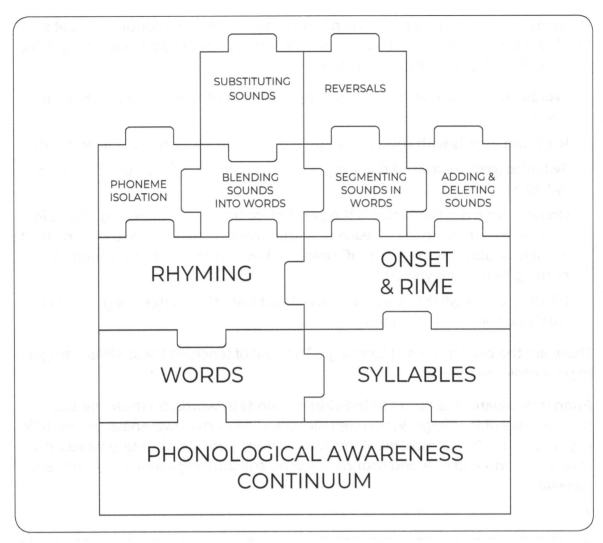

Building blocks of literacy

It is also helpful to define the term *phoneme*. There are a ton of fancy terms when you start really digging into the science of how we read, but we like to break them all down and make it as easy as possible for everyone to understand.

A phoneme is the smallest unit of sound. Let's take a look at the word "shark," for example. There are three phonemes (or sounds) in the word shark, /sh/ /ar/ /k/. When you see the term phoneme, just think "sounds."

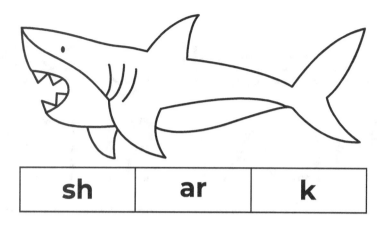

| sh | ar | k |

> **Reading problems can be prevented if all students are trained in letter-sound skills and phonological awareness. —David Kilpatrick**

The PA Skills

These are the skills that build phonological and phonemic awareness. We'll describe them in the coming pages:

Phonological awareness skills

Word awareness/concept of word

Syllable awareness

Rhyme

Onset and rime

Phonemic awareness skills

Phoneme isolation

Phoneme blending

Phoneme segmenting

Advanced phonemic awareness skills

Phoneme addition

Phoneme/syllable deletion

Phoneme substitution

Bonus skills

Bonus 1: Advanced phoneme manipulation

Bonus 2: Reversals

Pre-reading Skills
CHEAT SHEET

Phonological Awareness:

1. Word Awareness (hearing words in sentences)
2. Syllables
3. Rhyming
4. Onset and Rime

The goal of the above skills is to get to the skills below.

Phonemic Awareness

(the next part of phonological awareness):

5. Phoneme Isolation (beginning, ending, middle sounds)
6. Phoneme Blending (say each sound in a word and have the child blend)
7. Phoneme Segmentation (say a word and have the child segment sounds)
8. Phoneme Addition (add a sound to a word)
9. Phoneme Deletion (take away a sound in a word)
10. Phoneme Substitution (change sounds in a word)

@droppinknowledgewithheidi

Phonological Awareness

Let's dive a little bit deeper into phonological awareness. Typically the skills covered here are words in sentences, rhyming, syllables, and onset and rime.

The goal of these early phonological awareness skills is to get to phonemic awareness!

Sometimes when we hear that foundational skills such as phonological awareness are crucial to help building a strong base for kids to begin to read, we become focused on getting our kids to *master* these skills. But as discussed previously, the goal of early phonological awareness is to get to phonemic awareness. We want to make sure we are not belaboring these skills to get our kids to mastery. They are great starting points and should be practiced to help progress students along, but we don't want to be stuck working on rhyming words or syllable division for weeks because our students are still struggling with these concepts. We want to continue to move on to phonemic awareness skills, because this is where we will gain the most ground in getting our kids to read.

Step 1: Phonological Awareness
Word Awareness/Concept of Word

Why does word awareness matter? Learning to read is all about sounds. Knowing that words are part of the sentences we speak every day is the first step to recognizing patterns in language.

To practice:
- Say a complete sentence (in your natural speaking voice).
- Have your child repeat the sentence.
- Have your child count the number of words in that sentence.

Tips:
- Repeat the sentence as needed.
- Model how you count the words if your child is having trouble.
- Add movement! Stomp, clap, or jump out the words.
- Do this anytime of the day. When you say normal things such as "Pick up your toys, please," ask your child how many words were in your sentence.
- Incorporate fidget tools!
- This is a great skill to practice on a walk or on a car ride!
- Use building blocks! One block for each word they hear.

Sample Sentences:

Beginner sentences have words with one syllable. Intermediate sentences have multisyllabic words. Often, it is tricky for younger children to count multisyllabic words as one word in this activity.

Beginner	Intermediate
We went to the store.	My family drove to the store yesterday.
Did you see the bird?	Did you see the eagle in the sky?
The bear can sleep.	The bear hibernates in the winter.
It's time for a bath.	She was splashing in the bathtub!
The tree is green.	The leaves are falling off of the tree.
He can bounce the ball.	He is bouncing the basketball.
That card is nice.	We are making a card for grandma!
It is spring!	I see flowers and butterflies.
I like to ride my bike.	He was riding his bike on a sunny day.
We play with our friends.	(Name) was playing Monopoly yesterday.
Thank you for the note.	Thank you for picking up that tractor.
What time is it?	At 10 o'clock we are going to (place).
I like to play with my toys.	Play-Doh is my favorite activity.
The stove is hot.	We were cooking in the kitchen.
Let's roll the dice!	The dice landed on the number one!
I can see the duck.	I need glasses to read this story.
We like to cut out shapes.	We use scissors to cut out rectangles.
My coat is blue.	My jacket is purple, and it has a zipper.
I like to drink milk.	My favorite drink is lemonade.
Can you write this word?	We are writing a sentence in the notebook.
Let's go to the park.	Are you ready to play soccer at the park?

Step 2: Phonological Awareness
Syllable Awareness

A syllable is technically "a unit of pronunciation having one vowel sound, with or without surrounding consonants, forming the whole or a part of a word" but when teaching my students, we say a syllable is like a beat.

Another trick for teaching syllables is that each vowel is a syllable. Vowel sounds make your mouth open. So, each time your mouth opens (or your chin drops), that's a syllable!

To practice:
- Say a word.
- Have your child repeat the word.
- Have your child count the number of syllables in that word.

Blending:
- Say a word but pause at the syllables.
- Have your child tell you what word it is.

Segmenting:
- Say a 2+ syllable word.
- Have your child break that word at the syllables.

Tips:
- Repeat the word as needed.
- Model how you count the syllables if your child is having trouble.
- Add movement! Stomp, clap, or jump out the syllables.
- Keep in mind that this takes practice. Many times, a child will tend to draw out words to add extra syllables (e.g. CH – AIR rather than chair).
- Consistent practice is key.
- Have your child hold their hand under their chin to feel when their mouth opens, or chin drops, when saying a word.
- Play during dinner, bath time, or playtime!
- Use Play-Doh to "smash" the syllables!
- With blending and segmenting, it is easiest to start with compound words!

Sample Words:

1 Syllable	2 Syllables	3 Syllables
park	table	spaghetti
ride	roller	computer
go	fable	unicorn
plant	sister	dinosaur
cup	tumble	banana
maze	sweaty	eleven
rise	lemon	celebrate
soup	windy	chocolate
red	little	elephant
bike	zebra	energy
sky	frosty	amazing
stamp	silly	memory
through	finger	together
scarf	window	envelope
mind	flower	Africa
cup	cousin	holiday
stairs	frozen	forever
light	sticky	dangerous
stay	monkey	ultimate
good	waffle	important
home	playing	potato
wolf	reindeer	happiness

Sample Words:

Blending

sun – shine	rain – bow	good – bye
cow – boy	bow – tie	cup – cake
tooth – brush	pan – cake	cat – fish
ear – ring	snow – man	sun – light
hot – dog	base – ball	note – book
ha – ppy	car – rot	ap – ple
let – ter	bun – ny	pen – cil
ma – gic	win – dy	sis – ter
le – mon	su – per	ta – ble

Segmenting

sandpit	Sunday	napkin
armchair	bedroom	bookcase
ballpark	carpool	earthquake
daybed	bellhop	teapot
tadpole	toolbox	sidewalk
seashore	sidekick	someone
contest	public	summer
muffin	signal	problem
thunder	winner	slippers

Step 3: Phonological Awareness Rhyme

There is a progression to learning rhyme. It is easier for a child to identify rhyming words than it is to produce a rhyme. If your child is having a hard time producing a rhyming word, continue to work on rhyme recognition.

To practice rhyme recognition:
* Say two words (sometimes rhyming words, sometimes non-rhyming words). Ask your child if those words rhyme or not.

To practice rhyme production:
* Say a word. Have your child come up with a word that rhymes.

Tips:
* Nonsense words count!
* Model for your child as needed.
* Remind them that rhyming words have the same ENDING sound.
* Use your hands for a visual. For example, if your words are snow and go, push one fist forward for /sn/ and the other for /o/, then say go and push one fist forward for /g/ and the other for /o/. This gives them a visual for the ending sounds.
* Use thumbs up/thumbs down.
* Add toys! While your child is playing, use the names of their toys to practice rhyming.
* Practice in the car!
* If they are just not getting rhyming, move on!

"Students who are weak on indicators of phonological awareness development will benefit most from instruction aimed at systematic strengthening of the skills that are most closely related to understanding how letters represent spoken language. While rhyming might be in the mix, the tasks with the biggest pay-off will be those focused on phonemes." —Louisa Moats[4]

---

[4]https://improvingliteracy.org/ask-an-expert/must-children-master-rhyming-being-taught-recognize-segment-blend-and-manipulate/.

Sample Words for Rhyme Recognition:

pack – back	sting – ring	go – from
plant – green	glass – glad	make – take
ball – fall	play – push	light – night
rain – cane	bat – ring	hair – bear
marker – crayon	snow – show	coat – boat
fly – cry	ten – nine	you – shoe
floor – more	ride – side	street – road
clip – chip	run – hat	yellow – flower
horse – zebra	call – tall	bend – send
time – winter	bat – flat	big – small

Sample Words for Rhyme Production:

not	tap	too
cat	pan	ride
wall	sing	rang
mitt	toe	care
map	car	leaf
net	shoe	tree
snip	horn	toad
chop	cup	green

Step 4: Phonological Awareness Onset and Rime

Many times, people think that rime is the same as rhyme, but it is not. Onset refers to the first phonological unit of a word. Basically, onset refers to the consonants before the vowel in a word. The rime is the string of letters that follow.

For example:
PL is the onset – ANT is the rime (PLANT)
SPL is the onset – IT is the rime (SPLIT)
SH is the onset – ARK is the rime (SHARK)
C is the onset – AT is the rime (CAT)

To practice onset and rime:
- Say the onset of a word, pause, then say the rest of the word.
- Ask your child what word that is.

Tips:
- Model for your child as needed.
- Remember to pause in between sounds.
- Do this when giving directions or talking with your child.
- Stick with one-syllable words when working on this skill.
- Do not show your child the written words.
- Use words that represent things your child is interested in.
- Practice this while your child plays!
- This is a great game to play in the car. Use words of things you see outside!
- Use toys to practice these first four skills!

*Fun Fact: Not all words have onsets! Single syllable words that start with a vowel (ill, ax, ear, oar) do not have an onset.

Sample Words:

sh – ark	t – ab	r – un
m – eet	sh – out	b – all
h – ead	h – orn	d – ip
w – atch	th – ink	ch – ore
b – ud	l – amp	p – ig
m – arch	sh – ape	c – ake
f – ork	sl – ice	sh – eep
fl – ag	m – int	j – oke
r – ain	v – est	r – ose
h – eart	l – east	f – irst
g – ap	t – each	r – ead
p – ink	spl – ash	tr – uck
f – air	g – et	p – aint
b – est	y – arn	n – eck
s – and	sh – ake	shr – imp
m – ake	th – ing	f – old
h – ang	wh – ale	k – ick
t – ape	ch – omp	ph – one

Phonemic Awareness

Phonemic awareness includes the beginning PA skills such as isolating, blending, and segmenting sounds. Then, we move to more advanced PA skills that include adding sounds, deleting sounds, substituting sounds, and reversing sounds. Let's talk about each of these skills.

Step 5: Phonemic Awareness
Phoneme Isolation

Remember that phoneme simply means sound. In this activity, you want your child to be able to identify SOUNDS (not letters) in spoken words.

It is important to note that you want them to tell you the sound, not the letter. For example, if you say the word HOME and ask them what the first sound is, you want them to say the sound H makes, /h/, not tell you the letter H. They do not need to know their letter names to do this activity.

To practice phoneme isolation:
- Say a word.
- Have your child repeat that word.
- Ask your child what sound they heard at the beginning, middle, or end of that word.

Tips:
- Start with just beginning sounds. This is typically the easiest for them to hear.
- Then work on ending sounds.
- Then work on middle sounds.
- Use alliteration!
- When your child can recognize these sounds, mix it up and eventually ask them to tell you the beginning, middle, and ending sounds in each word.

Sample Words for Beginning Sounds:

cat /k/	boy /b/	get /g/	fun /f/	soar /s/
hat /h/	crown /k/	part /p/	thing /th/	home /h/
car /k/	road /r/	sing /s/	never /n/	otter /o/
bike /b/	sheep /sh/	swim /s/	guess /g/	love /l/
pop /p/	rain /r/	chip /ch/	dance /d/	shoe /sh/
tape /t/	yard /y/	apple /a/	work /w/	mix /m/

Sample Words for Middle Sounds:

crumb /u/	man /a/	sit /i/	pop /o/	cup /u/
sip /i/	lap /a/	get /e/	ship /i/	mat /a/
mom /o/	pup /u/	tap /a/	net /e/	pin /i/
stop /o/	ten /e/	miss /i/	fan /a/	step /e/
pit /i/	hop /o/	run /u/	mesh /e/	fat /a/
when /e/	quit /i/	lot /o/	sun /u/	zip /i/

Sample Words for Ending Sounds:

bake /k/	make /k/	lean /n/	tab /b/	from /m/
said /d/	farm /m/	nest /t/	tag /g/	blue /oo/
truck /k/	glass /s/	bike /k/	best /t/	stuck /k/
hand /d/	where /r/	fall /l/	room /m/	have /v/
dine /n/	push /sh/	zip /p/	reach /ch/	front /t/
little /l/	furry /ee/	book /k/	late /t/	round /d/

Step 6: Phonemic Awareness Phoneme Blending

When you are working on blending, you want your child to hear the sounds of a word and blend them together to say the word.

To practice phoneme blending:
- Say the sounds of a word.
- Have your child repeat the sounds.
- Tell your child to say it fast and blend the sounds together.

Tips:
- Repeat the sounds of the word if necessary.
- Start with two sound words, then move to three sound words, then four sound words, etc.

Step 7: Phonemic Awareness Phoneme Segmenting

Segmenting is the opposite of blending. Now you want your child to be able to take that word apart!

To practice phoneme segmenting:
- Say a word.
- Have your child repeat the word.
- Now ask your child to say each sound of the word.

Tips:
- Repeat the word if necessary.
- Do this with your child the first couple of times.
- Start with two sound words, then move to three sound words, then four sound words, etc.

Sample Words for Blending & Segmenting:

Blending	Segmenting
/m/ - /a/ - /n/	man
/c/ - /a/ - /t/	cat
/l/ - /i/ - /n/ - /t/	lint
/s/ - /e/ - /n/ - /d/	send
/m/ - /i/ - /s/	miss
/sh/ - /i/ - /p/	ship
/y/ - /ar/ - /d/	yard
/k/ - /i/ - /k/	kick
/b/ - /a/ - /th/	bath
/t/ - /o/ - /p/	top
/g/ - /r/ - /ee/ - /n/	green
/s/ - /e/ - /d/	said
/s/ - /l/ - /ee/ - /p/	sleep
/p/ - /o/ - /n/ - /d/	pond
/f/ - /l/ - /a/ - /g/	flag
/t/ - /r/ - /u/ - /k/	truck
/t/ - /u/ - /f/	tough
/r/ - /i/ - /p/ - /t/	ripped
/ch/ - /i/ - /l/	chill

The following pages can be used for more practice with phonemic awareness. Simply print, laminate, and cut the cards. You can use these for identifying and isolating beginning, middle, and/or ending sounds. You can also use them for practice segmenting sounds. Place in a center with any manipulatives for kids to place in the boxes as they break apart each word.

Pro-tip: Use magnetic letters as the manipulative so kids are making those sound–symbol connections! And by incorporating manipulatives into your practice you are providing multimodality instruction, which can enhance your students' ability to make that sound–symbol connection in their reading brain.

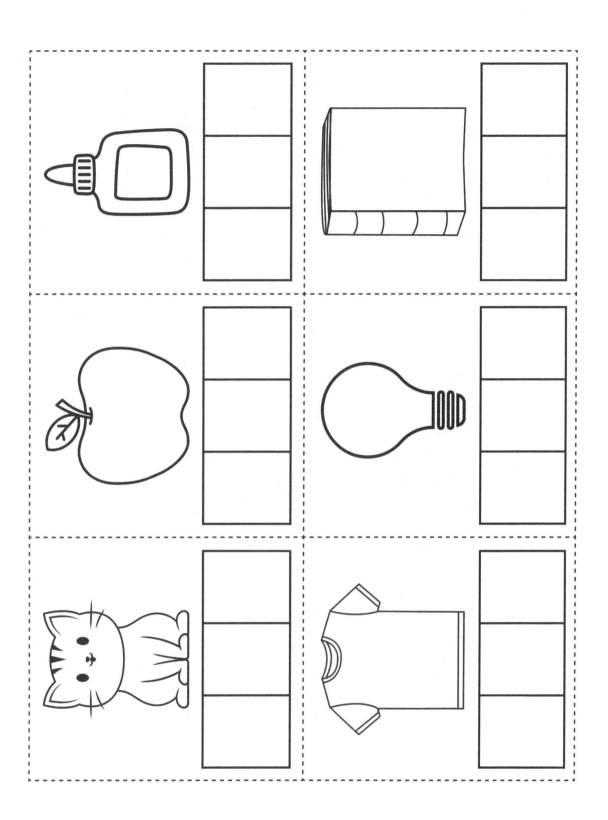

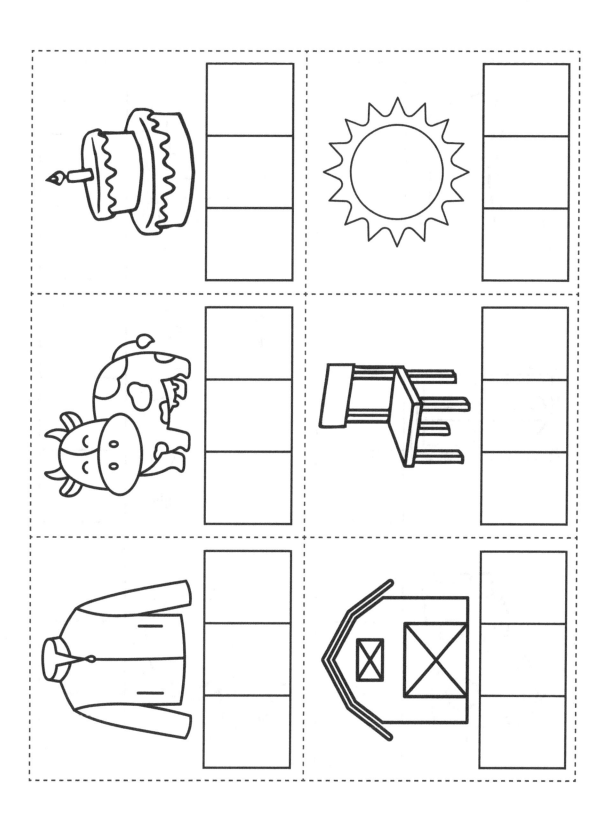

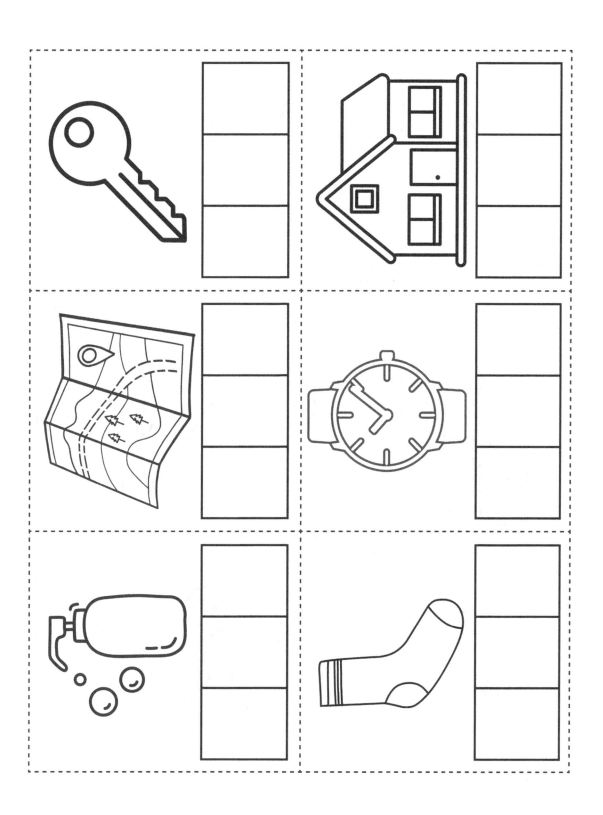

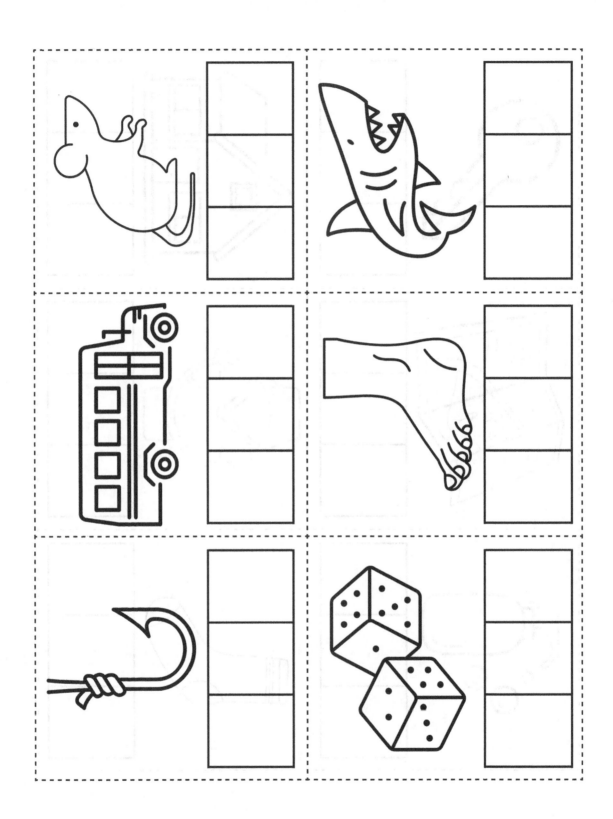

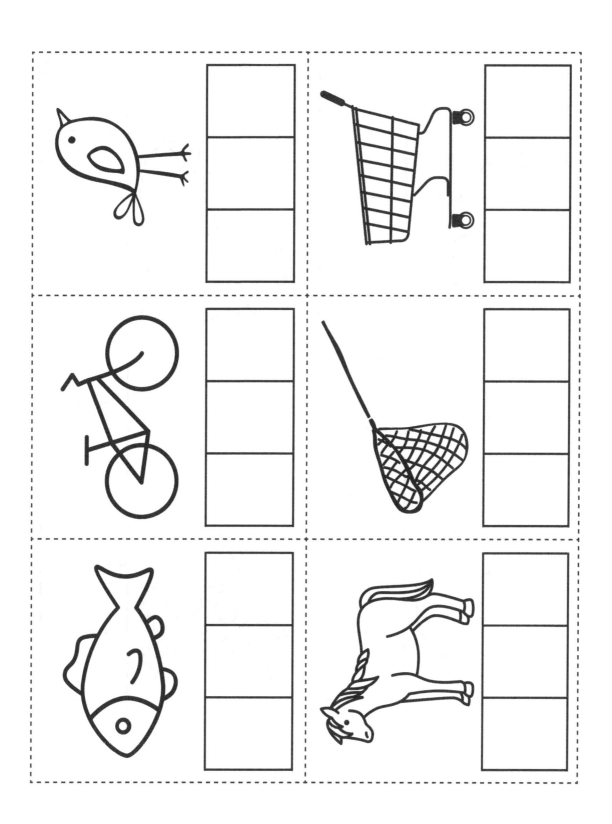

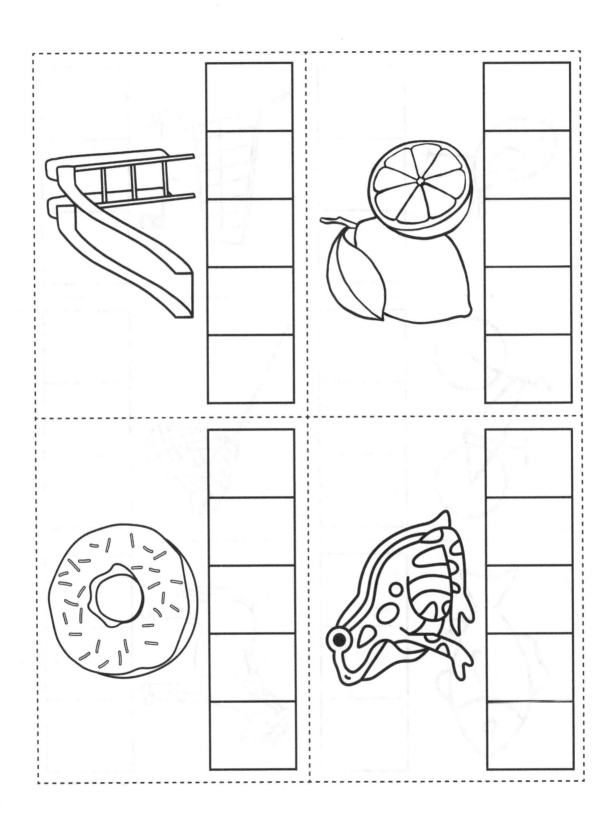

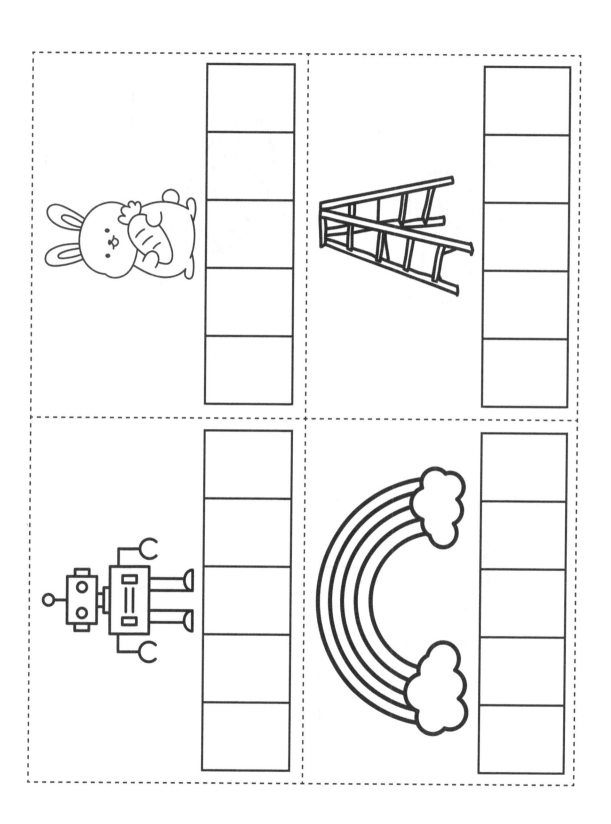

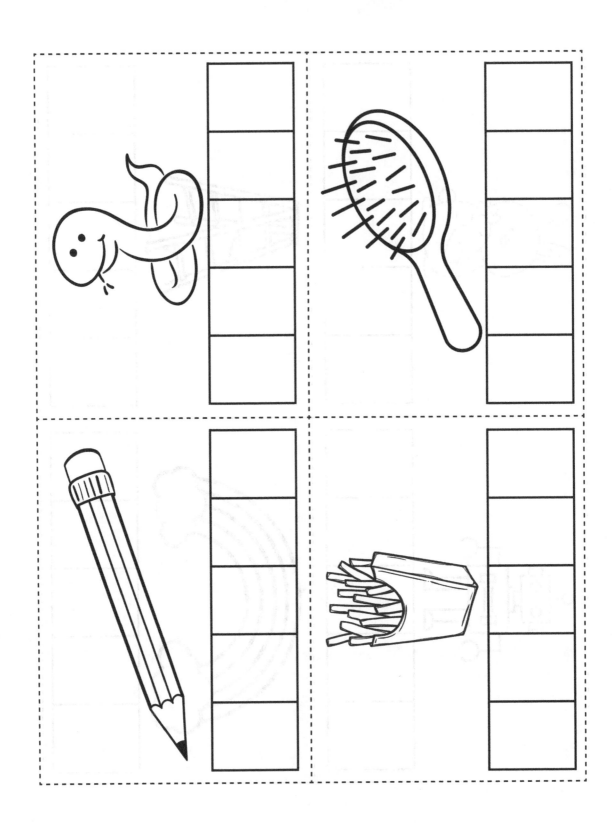

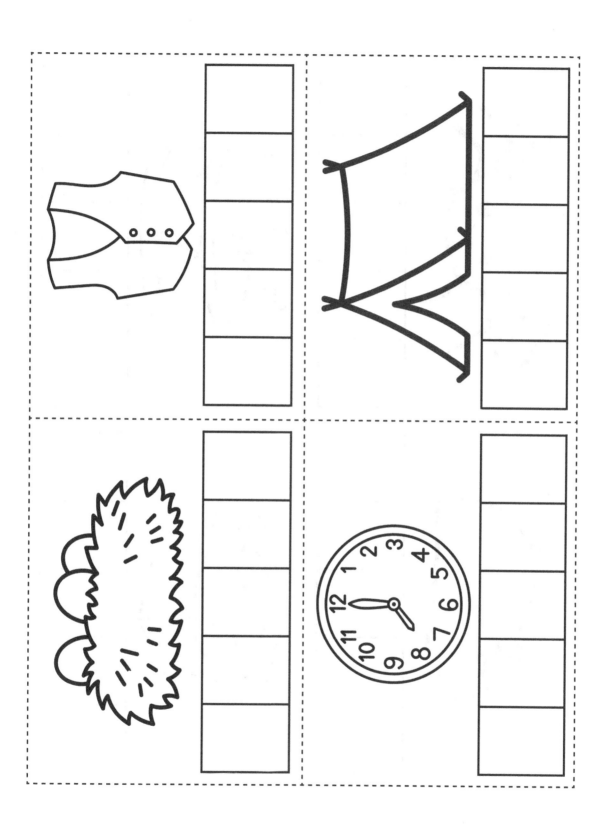

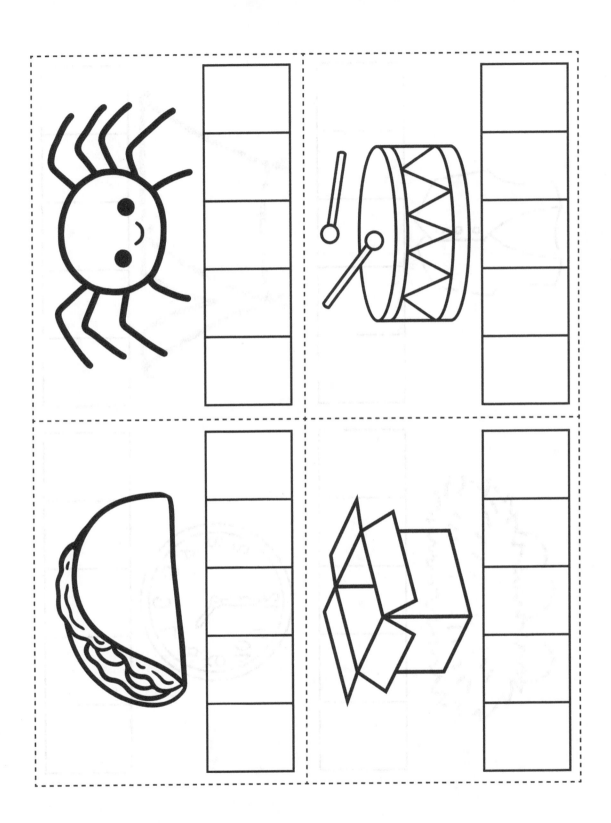

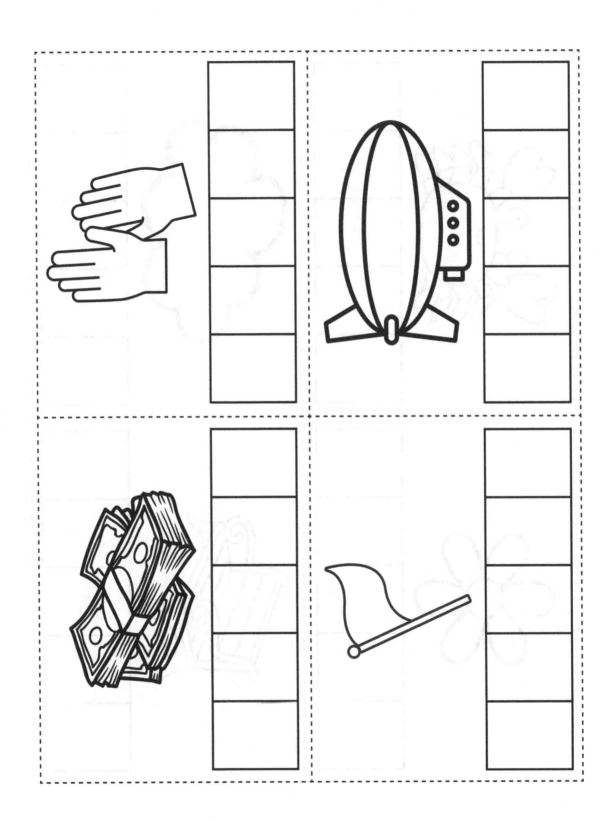

Congratulations! The Advanced Skills!

You have made it to the advanced portion of phonemic awareness! Some researchers argue that these skills are not necessary for students to be successful readers. While we do not have the answer for you, we can tell you that our own children and students do find these skills fun to practice. **We do not dedicate a ton of instructional time to these skills**, but they can be fun to practice when kids are ready, and if you have extra time.

Typically, advanced phonemic awareness skills would not be taught until late first grade and into second and third grade. However, if you have a child who is proficient with the skills we discussed previously, you could try working with them on some of the following skills.

Step 8: Phonemic Awareness Phoneme Addition

Congratulations! You have made it to the advanced portion of phonemic awareness! These skills are often more difficult for children to master but are just as important in building a strong foundation for reading.

Phoneme Addition simply means we are going to add a sound to our words. For example, I might say BELL but ask my child to add a /t/ (sound, not letter) to the end to make the word BELT.

To practice phoneme addition:
- Say a word.
- Have your child repeat the word.
- Now ask your child to add a sound (of your choice) to the word.

Tips:
- Repeat the word if necessary.
- Do this with your child the first couple times.
- Play this game while your child is playing.
- Use names of toys or animals that your child likes.

Sample Words for Phoneme Addition:

Say	Add to BEGINNING of word	New word
top	/s/	stop
and	/b/	band
ear	/t/	tear
lip	/f/	flip
team	/s/	steam
pot	/s/	spot
trap	/s/	strap
mile	/s/	smile
lad	/g/	glad

Say	Add to END of word	New word
bell	/t/	belt
store	/ee/	story
mine	/d/	mind
star	/t/	start
plan	/t/	plant
bus	/t/	bust
pass	/t/	past
pin	/ch/	pinch
shell	/f/	shelf

Step 9: Phonemic Awareness Phoneme/Syllable Deletion

Opposite of Phoneme Addition, this time we are going to take away a sound or a syllable!

To practice phoneme/syllable deletion:
- Say a word.
- Have your child repeat the word.
- Now ask your child to say that word again, but don't say (sound or syllable of your choice). For example, have your child say CHAIR, and ask them to say it again but don't say /ch/. The answer would be AIR.

Tips:
- Model this as needed.
- Repeat the sounds of the word as needed.
- When first starting this, emphasizing the sound that should stay can be helpful. For example, if you are doing a word like robot, and having your child take away the RO, then emphasize BOT when you say the word.
- Use words from around the house.
- Use names of their favorite things.

Sample Words for Phoneme/Syllable Deletion:

Say...	Now say it again without the...	Answer:
lunch	/ch/	lun
robot	/row/	bot
garden	/gar/	den
snow	/s/	no
chair	/ch/	air
slip	/s/	lip
table	/tay/	bull
stuck	/st/	uck
jacket	/kit/	jack
grow	/g/	row
peach	/ch/	pea
winter	/ter/	win
think	/th/	ink
sheep	/sh/	eep
sticker	/er/	stick
munch	/ch/	mun
sweet	/s/	weet
center	/sen/	ter
gold	/g/	old

Step 10: Phonemic Awareness Phoneme Substitution

In this activity, you are asking children to change sounds in words to make new words. This can be difficult at first.

To practice phoneme substitution:
- Say a word.
- Have your child repeat the word.
- Now ask your child to change one of the sounds in the word.
- Have them tell you the new word.

Tips:
- Start with changing beginning sounds.
- Then move to ending sounds.
- Then move to middle sounds.
- Repeat sounds as necessary but do not use print.
- Model first if needed. For example, say hat, bat and emphasize the beginning sounds so your child can hear the difference. Repeat sounds if needed.

Sample Words for Beginning Sounds:

Say...	Change...	New word	Say...	Change...	New Word
hat	/h/ to /b/	bat	thing	/th/ to /r/	ring
car	/c/ to /f/	far	chip	/ch/ to /t/	tip
bike	/b/ to /l/	like	guess	/g/ to /m/	mess
pop	/p/ to /fl/	flop	dance	/d/ to /pr/	prance
ten	/t/ to /w/	when	park	/p/ to /sh/	shark

Sample Words for Ending Sounds:

Say...	Change...	New word	Say...	Change...	New Word
bat	/t/ to /m/	bam	roll	/l/ to /m/	roam
cape	/p/ to /m/	came	sharp	/p/ to /k/	shark
cup	/p/ to /t/	cut	park	/k/ to /t/	part
home	/m/ to /p/	hope	chill	/l/ to /p/	chip
drain	/n/ to /p/	drape	phone	/n/ to /m/	foam

Sample Words for Middle Sounds:

Say...	Change...	New word	Say...	Change...	New Word
fat	/a/ to /i/	fit	song	/o/ to /u/	sung
run	/u/ to /a/	ran	chip	/i/ to /o/	chop
kit	/i/ to /u/	cut	fin	/i/ to /a/	fan
pop	/o/ to /u/	pup	then	/e/ to /a/	than
ten	/e/ to /a/	tan	moon	/oo/ to /a/	man

Bonus 1: Advanced Phoneme Manipulation

As your child or students become more familiar with these skills, you can continue to refine these skills with advanced phoneme manipulation. This involves changing or deleting a sound in the middle of a word.

To practice phoneme/syllable:
- Say a word.
- Have your child repeat the word.
- Now ask your child to change or delete a sound
- Have them tell you the new word.

Deletion:

Say...	Now say it again without the...	Answer:
nest	/s/	net
spy	/p/	sigh
string	/r/	sting
brag	/r/	bag

Substitution:

Say...	Change...	New word	Say...	Change...	New Word
test	/s/ to /n/	tent	braid	/r/ to /l/	blade
play	/l/ to /r/	pray	flows	/l/ to /r/	froze
spell	/p/ to /m/	smell	other	/th/ to /sh/	usher

Bonus 2: Reversals

To practice this skill, you give the child a word and then ask them to reverse the sounds. For example, if I say tap and then ask you to reverse it, the new word would be pat.

It can be helpful to incorporate letters for this task but be careful when the spelling changes!

Say...	Now reverse it...
pat	tap
bad	dab
tip	pit
bit	tib
cab	back
pod	dop
tag	gat
lip	pill
pad	dap
sap	pass
bat	tab
jab	badge

Cue Cards

Printable cards you can take with you wherever you go!

Word Awareness:

- He can run so fast! (5)
- Can you see the bird? (5)
- I love you. (3)
- We like to ride our bikes. (6)
- That tree is huge! (4)
- I see a cloud in the sky. (7)
- How are you today? (4)
- We see tigers at the zoo. (6)
- Can you reach the top? (5)
- It is time for dinner! (5)
- She can go to the store. (6)
- We love to play checkers. (5)
- The ducks are swimming. (4)
- I will write a letter. (5)
- The sun is shining! (4)
- He needs glasses to see. (5)

Syllables:

plant	fog
telephone	elevator
pillow	nurse
truck	butterfly
monster	pizza
sand	light
stairs	counting
garbage	last
Sunday	lemonade
pencil	month
elephant	tape
happiness	koala
furry	sunny
slide	blue
grumpy	clean
brown	ladder

Rhyming 1: Does it rhyme?

hand – sand	wood – could
go – stop	still – spoon
lumpy – bumpy	rain – gain
pen – gem	card – yard
glad – sad	kid – cold
ran – map	ten – men
blue – shoe	spoon – moon
now – cow	tree – sky
black – floor	page – note
hole – bowl	two – new
nose – ride	heart – start
kite – bite	can – span
fur – far	ring – sing
meat – team	stuck – start
eye – bye	we – see
flash – mash	look – hook

Rhyming 2: Which words rhyme?

- bite – kite – book
- shark – shut – hut
- pile – pants – style
- pen – hen – hand
- white – harp – sharp
- them – stem – stew
- walk – run – stalk
- salt – fault – pot
- toe – jump – go
- cloud – ball – tall
- pink – frog – stink
- shirt – hurt – stay
- green – two – mean
- cut – wall – mall
- chip – chop – ship
- chart – heart - mine

Cue Cards

Rhyming 3: Find a word that rhymes…		Onset and Rime	
spoon	net	gr – eat	fr – og
train	white	gl – ad	sp – oon
cart	ant	fr – om	b – ake
mind	blue	sh – ed	ch – ore
land	crown	b – ark	f – ork
sing	big	s – and	r – ug
trip	oat	cr – awl	st – ick
hot	chunk	m – ail	gr – een
chat	clock	h – ill	ch – ick
mitt	sick	b – ird	p – ants
shut	pack	j – ump	h – air
when	mark	wh – ale	w – ent
went	there	str – aight	r – ed
bring	rail	f – ine	th – ing
run	sky	m – eet	p – ot
ice	shine	c – old	n – et

Phonemic Awareness: Isolation (Beg, Mid, or End)		Phonemic Awareness: Blending and Segmenting	
sand	still	/h/ - /ar/ - /t/	heart
stop	gain	/s/ - /u/ - /n/	sun
bump	yard	/b/ - /a/ - /k/	back
gem	kid	/k/ - /i/ - /k/	kick
glad	men	/p/ - /e/ - /n/	pen
map	note	/n/ - /a/ - /p/	nap
black	can	/f/ - /u/ - /n/	fun
ride	stuck	/r/ - /e/ - /d/	red
nose	cat	/l/ - /e/ - /g/	leg
bite	home	/m/ - /a/ - /t/	mat
team	light	/h/ - /a/ - /v/	have
flash	pack	/j/ - /a/ - /m/	jam
start	wall	/k/ - /u/ - /t/	cut
shake	pile	/h/ - /i/ - /d/	hid
moon	chop	/w/ - /a/ - /g/	wag
tan	mine	/t/ - /a/ - /p/	tap

Cue Cards

Phonemic Awareness: Addition	Phonemic Awareness: Deletion
Say grow, add /n/ to the end (grown)	Say store but don't say /st/ (or)
Say hi, add /d/ to the end (hide)	Say great but don't say /gr/ (ate)
Say row, add /st/ to the end (roast)	Say hat but don't say /h/ (at)
Say why, add /l/ to the end (while)	Say friend but don't say /fr/ (end)
Say me, add /t/ to the end (meet)	Say chair but don't say /ch/ (air)
Say car, add /d/ to the end (card)	Say snow but don't say /s/ (no)
Say hair, add /ee/ to the end (hairy)	Say card but don't say /d/ (car)
Say flow, add /t/ to the end (float)	Say plant but don't say /t/ (plan)
Say lad, add /g/ to the beg. (glad)	Say mark but don't say /k/ (mar)
Say row, add /th/ to the beg. (throw)	Say books but don't say /s/ (book)
Say art, add /st/ to the beg. (start)	Say white but don't say /t/ (why)
Say ring, add /b/ to the beg. (bring)	Say tired but don't say /d/ (tire)
Say can, add /s/ to the beg. (scan)	Say reindeer but don't say rein (deer)
Say tale, add /s/ to the beg. (stale)	Say cupcake but don't say cake (cup)
Say ink, add /th/ to the beg. (think)	Say sunrise but don't say sun (rise)
Say right, add /b/ to the beg. (bright)	Say rainbow but don't say bow (rain)
Say top, add /s/ to the beg. (stop)	Say sailboat but don't say sail (boat)
Say ram, add /g/ to the beg. (gram)	Say earring but don't say ring (ear)

Phonemic Awareness: Substitution	Phonemic Awareness: Advanced
Say cat-change /c/ to /b/ (bat)	Say hand-don't say /n/ (had)
Say land-change /l/ to /s/ (sand)	Say pest-don't say /s/ (pet)
Say boys-change /b/ to /t/ (toys)	Say fact – don't say /k/ (fat)
Say pink-change /p/ to /th/ (think)	Say world-don't say /l/ (word)
Say map-change /m/ to /t/ (tap)	Say vent-don't say /n/ (vet)
Say dash-change /sh/ to /b/ (dab)	Say dusk-don't say /s/ (duck)
Say ride-change /d/ to /m/ (rhyme)	Say host-change /s/ to /p/ (hoped)
Say bird-change /d/ to /n/ (burn)	Say test-change /s/ to /n/ (tent)
Say pan-change /n/ to /t/ (pat)	Say pant-change /n/ to /s/ (past)
Say big-change /g/ to /n/ (bin)	Say bent-change /n/ to /s/ (best)
Say hat-change /a/ to /i/ (hit)	Say lift-change /f/ to /n/ (lint)
Say tab-change /a/ to /u/ (tub)	Say past-change /s/ to /n/ (pant)
Say fed-change /e/ to /oo/ (food)	Say wild-change /l/ to /n/ (wind)
Say mad-change /a/ to /u/ (mud)	Say fast-change /s/ to /k/ (fact)
Say road-change /oa/ to /i/ (rid)	Say next-change /ks/ to /s/ (nest)
Say sit-change /i/ to /a/ (sat)	Say mild-change /l/ to /n/ (mind)

Phonemic Awareness Can Be Done in the Dark ... But Should It Be?

You may have heard people say that phonological and phonemic awareness can be done in the dark. This is because it is an oral task. We want kids to be listening for sounds in words. However, there are benefits to using letters and connecting our phonemic awareness instruction to our phonics lessons.

https://droppinknowledge.com/droppin-knowledge-on-foundational-skills/

Why Should We Align Our Phonemic Awareness Instruction with Phonics?

The short answer is, this maximizes our instruction time! Phonemic awareness is usually taught as a warm-up at the beginning of a lesson. What better way to "warm up" than to get kids listening for the sounds they will be learning about in today's phonics lesson?

Let's take a look at the reading brain. Heidi developed this simplified version of the reading brain to make it easy to understand and also be able to share with your students.

When our brains read, we are connecting sounds to symbols. When we start our lessons with phonemic awareness, we activate our phonological processor (the part of our brains that processes sounds), and then we want to connect those sounds to the letters that represent them.

The **Simple** View of the Reading Brain

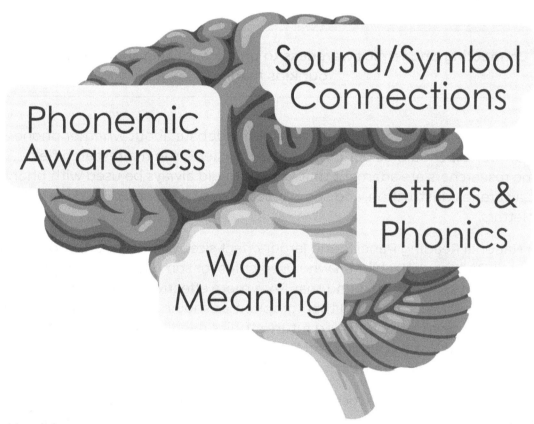

Sound/Symbol Connections

Phonemic Awareness

Letters & Phonics

Word Meaning

droppinknowledge.com

All of these parts must **work together** in order for us to read!

This begins the hardwiring (orthographic mapping) process that stores our words.

If we teach phonemic awareness separately from phonics, *we miss the chance to streamline the process* and make those connections. The faster we streamline this process, the more words we can start transferring to our kids' visual word form area. This is the area that stores the words we've decoded and know by sight, so that as soon as we see them we can read them without sounding them out or guessing. This creates more fluid reading and frees up space to begin comprehending what we are reading.

> **Connecting phonemic awareness to phonics is like a shortcut to getting our kids reading!**

At the time of writing this book, there is some debate about whether phonemic awareness should be done with or without letters in the research field. Some researchers are adamant that letters should always be used with phonemic awareness instruction, and some researchers say it should be done without letters.

The National Reading Panel found larger effect sizes with children who used letters with PA than with children who used chips (or some kind of manipulative). More recent research also found that PA is more effective with letters. This 2022 meta-analysis concluded that "graphemes should be incorporated into phonemic awareness instruction, and future studies need to provide information on dosage beyond just the length and frequency of sessions to clarify which aspects of these interventions are most efficient."[5]

We like to do both. We practice PA with letters when we are able to (and with older kids). We practice without letters when we are practicing on the go. There are many opportunities to incorporate PA in your daily lives and routines. That should not be missed.

---

[5] https://pubs.asha.org/doi/10.1044/2022_LSHSS-21-00160.

In the classroom, you can incorporate PA when giving instructions. For example, instead of saying take out your book, say take out your /b/ /oo/ /k/. When lining up, call students by sound. If your name starts with /s/, you may line up. If your name has a /d/ in it, you may line up. When you have three extra minutes before lunch, play I Spy. I spy something with the /sh/ sound.

At home, you can incorporate PA too! For example, instead of saying, please get a fork, say please get a /f/ /or/ /k/. When you are in the car, play I Spy. I spy something with the beginning sound /b/. When your child is playing, ask them what they are playing with and point out the sounds in that word. Go on a walk and find as many things as possible with the /g/ sound.

There are so many easy ways to incorporate phonemic awareness all day. Do not miss it just because you do not have letters available.

What About Older Students Who Are Struggling to Read?

If you have an older student who is having difficulty with reading, they may be missing the skills we just covered. Many times this is not discussed and is overlooked with older students since upper grades are working more on comprehension. This leads to older students getting tagged for their lack of comprehension skills, but the truth of the matter is, a lot of those struggling older students cannot decode the words in their texts. This usually relates to them lacking those foundational PA skills we just discussed.

Let's do a little example. Take a minute and read this passage.

At the Park

We are going to the park today. I will get my ?? and ?? so I can ?? ??. Tim will get his ?? and ?? so he can ??. Pam just ?? to go on the ??. Mom packed some ?? and then it was ?? to ??. I love the park!

This passage is shown at 80% accuracy. It may have been a little frustrating to read, right? Now, what if I asked you some comprehension questions?

● What did Tim get?

● What does Pam do?

- What did Mom pack?

- What happened at the park?

The problem for you is not comprehension, is it? The problem is that you cannot read the words!

Here, let's try this again...

At the Park

We are going to the park today. I will get my net and jar so I can catch bugs. Tim will get his ?? and ?? so he can ??. Pam just wants to go on the slide. Mom packed some snacks and then it was time to go. I love the park!

Much better, right? This passage is shown at around 95% accuracy.

But, what if one of my comprehension questions is "What did Tim get?"

Again, the issue is not comprehension here, it is the inability to read the words. While you can make your best guess, you don't really know, right? Some of our students are good guessers and some are not. However, we do not want them to guess. We want them to be able to read and decode. This exercise shows us that even at 95% accuracy, comprehension can still be affected. This is why it is important for us to assess and know our students' skill level when it comes to decoding.

Now, just because I know you are wondering . . . the actual words are "Tim will get his bat and ball so he can play."

So, if you have older kids who are struggling with comprehension, it is important to first make sure it is truly a comprehension issue, and not a decoding issue. When we get asked why a fourth grader is not able to decode, we usually suggest checking their phonemic awareness. Another problem teachers run into is that many of the resources available to teach this skill are intended for younger students.

The No Match Game

This is a game we developed where students will look at the pictures and find which one does not match based on *sounds*. You can use the illustrations on the following pages.

Note: To help older students with these skills, use *real photos*. Clip art can sometimes feel "childish" since many of the images are intended for primary school students. Doing the same activities but with *real* photos can help older students feel more confident.

The best part of this game is the conversations this can spark! We have shown these images to adults and had them get involved in some pretty great conversations around which answer they think is right and why! Kids can do the same and it is a great way to get kids working on foundational skills *plus* reasoning, background knowledge, vocabulary development, and speaking skills too!

For the image shown, some kids may choose the kite as the correct answer because the other images start with /l/ (light, lake, lime). Other kids may choose the lake as the correct answer because the other images have a long /l/ middle sound (light, lime, kite).

We don't tell students what each picture is. We leave it open for them to decide and come up with an answer based on their decisions. You will be surprised by the answers they come up with!

> **Remember, if the student knows their letters/phonics patterns, connecting sounds to symbols can fast-track those connections in their brains! Consider this when you are working on these skills with older students.**

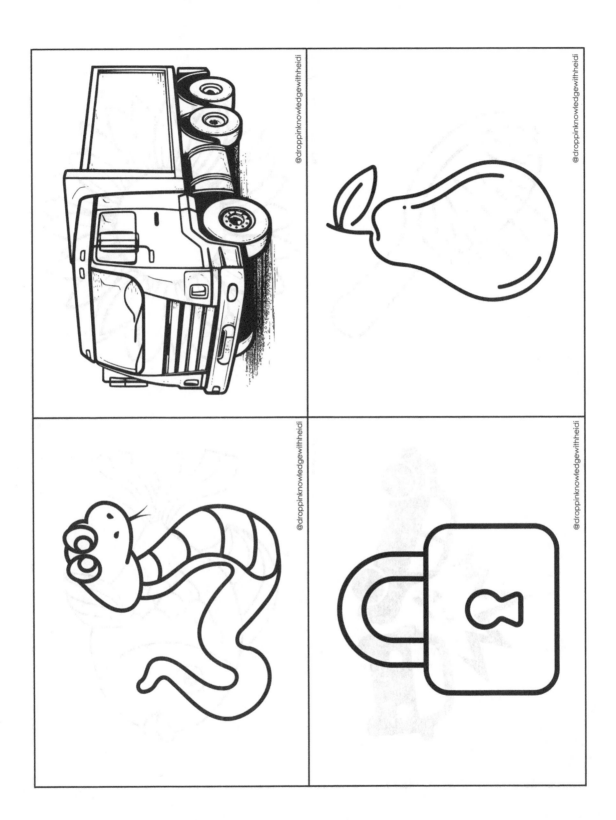

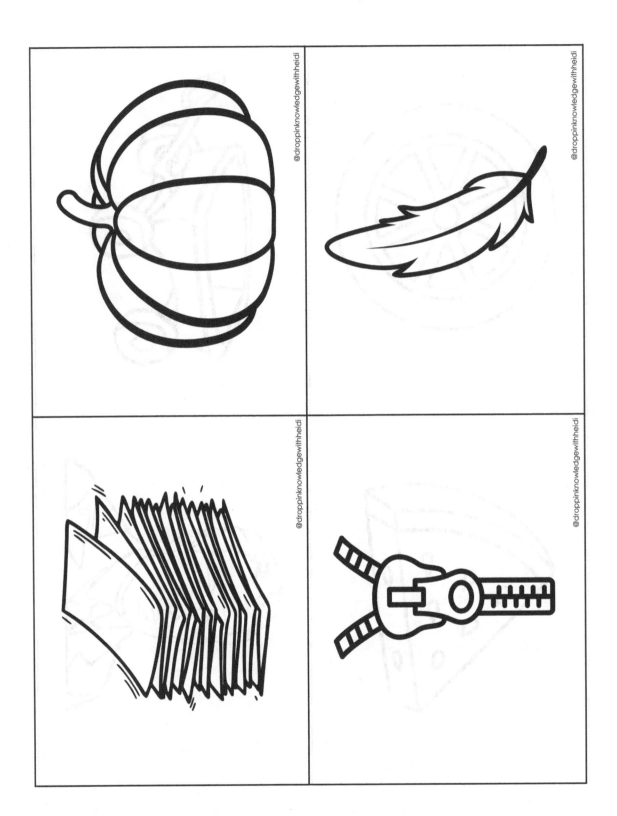

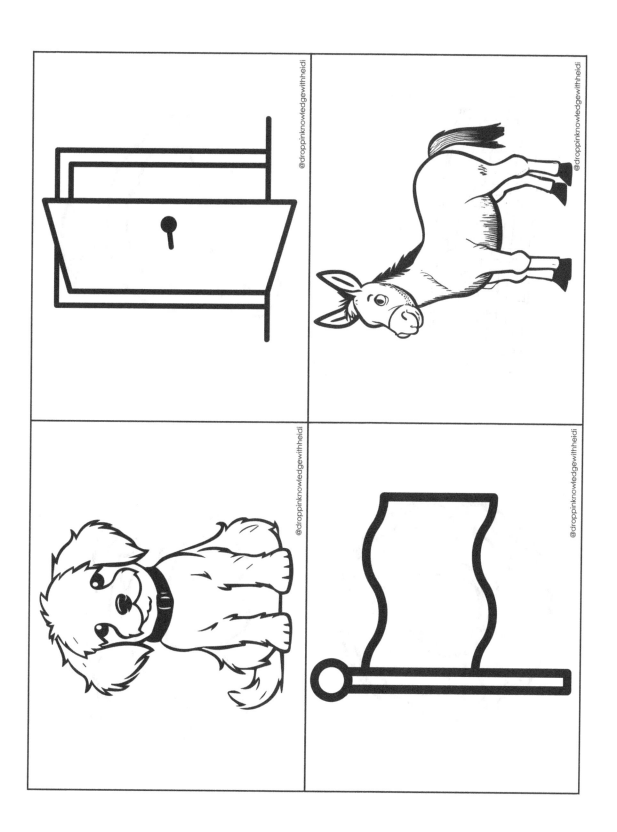

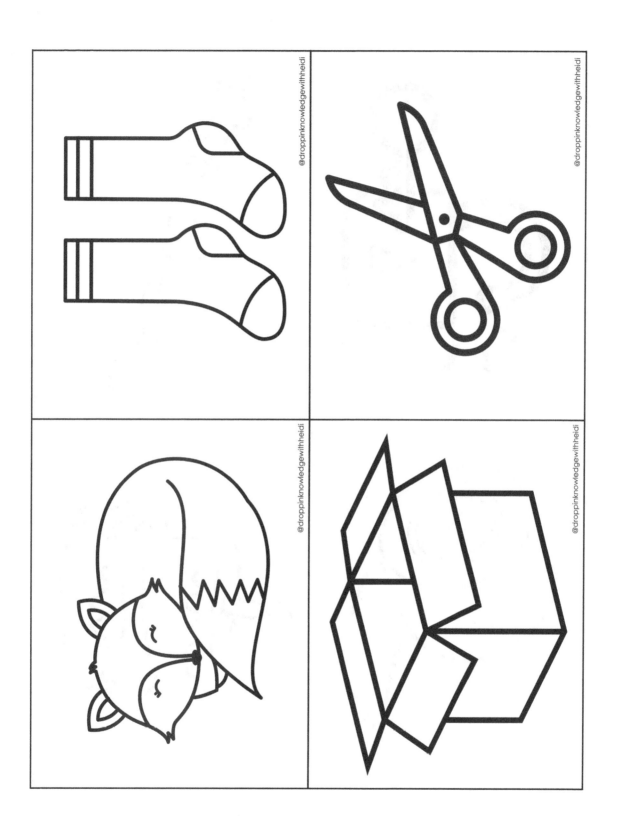

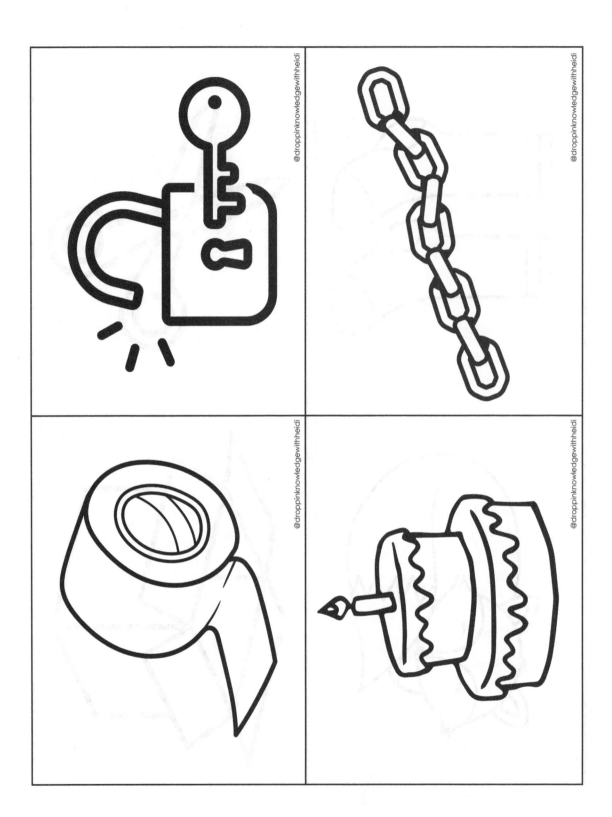

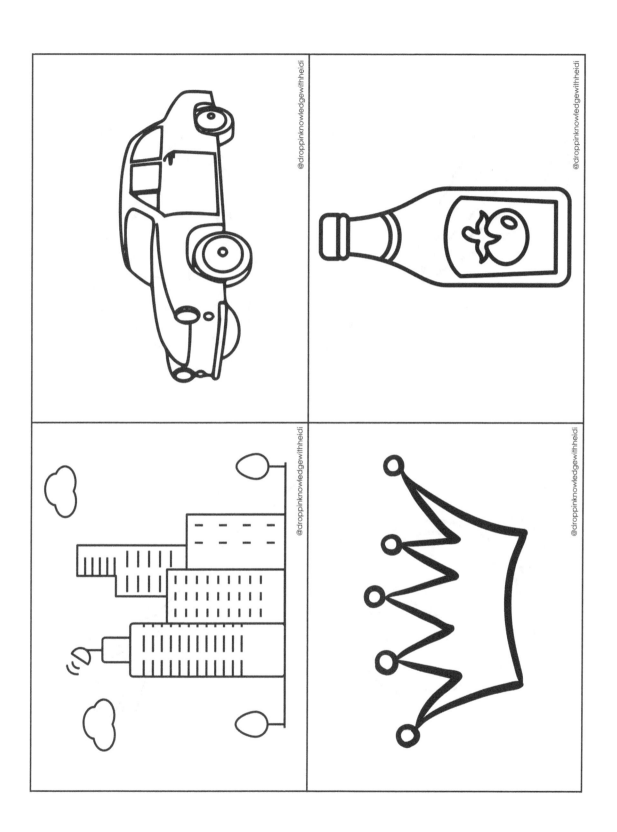

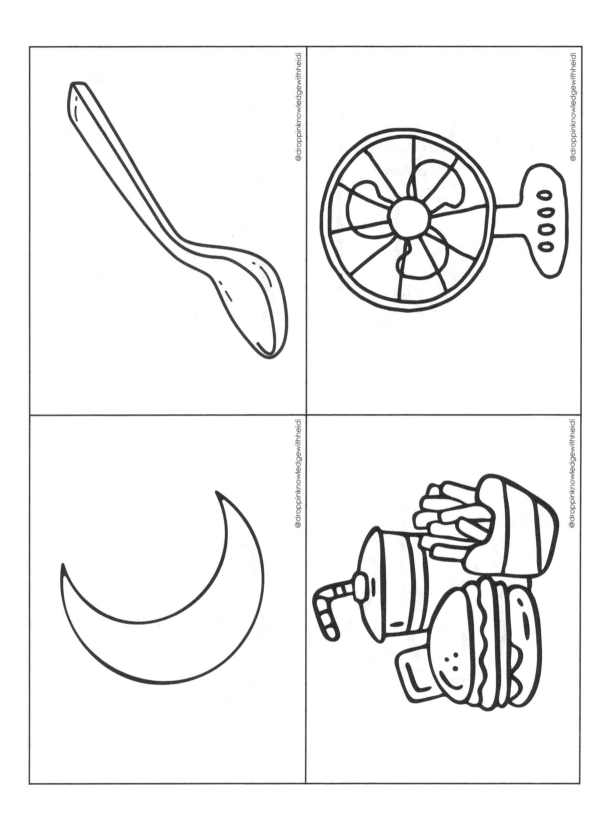

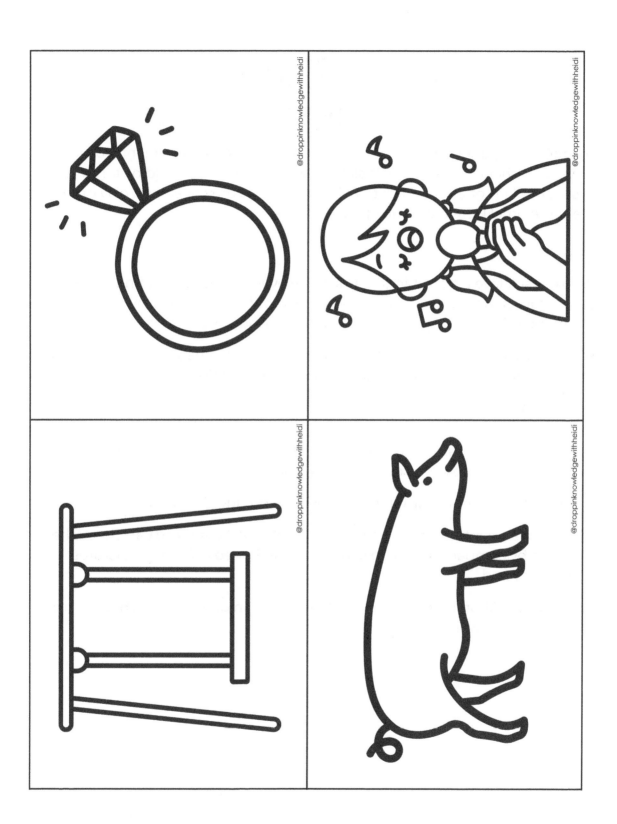

Bonus Phonemic Awareness Games

The following pages include games you can play with your students to work on various phonemic awareness skills. Learning can and should be fun! We can ensure our kids get the foundational reading skills they need and play games at the same time! Here are some of our favorites...

Bingo

Who doesn't love a good bingo game? However, we found that finding bingo games for phonemic awareness practice was difficult. That is why we created the Phoneme Addition Bingo and Phoneme Blending Bingo boards.

You can use the various bingo boards to help kids with beginning sound isolation, ending sound isolation, blending, and phoneme addition.

How to play:

1. Cut up the cue cards and place them all upside down. Give each student a bingo board. Flip over a cue card and read what it says.

2. Students will have to listen to the sounds and find the word.

3. Once a student gets five in a row, they call BINGO, and you can check their bingo by comparing the cue cards that are flipped over to the pictures they covered.

Phoneme Addition Bingo has two options. You can give students bingo cards with pictures or words.

/ă/	/b/	/k/	/d/
/ĕ/	/f/	/g/	/h/
/ĭ/	/j/	/l/	/m/
/n/	/ŏ/	/p/	/kw/
/r/	/s/	/t/	/ŭ/
/v/	/w/	/y/	/z/

Answer Key

/a/ - apple
/b/ - bear
/k/ - cupcake
/d/ - dice
/e/ - edge
/f/ - foot
/g/ - glue
/h/ - hammer
/i/ - igloo
/j/ - jellyfish
/l/ - llama
/m/ - map
/n/ - noodles
/o/ - octopus
/p/ - pretzel
/kw/ - queen
/r/ - ring
/s/ - scissors
/t/ - tie
/u/ - umbrella
/v/ - vest
/w/ - worm
/y/ - yarn
/z/ - zipper

*There is not a picture for x because at the beginning of words, x does not make its usual sound.

BINGO

BINGO

BINGO

BINGO

FREE
SPACE

@droppinknowledge.com

BINGO

BINGO

@droppinknowledge.com

BINGO

©droppinknowledge.com

BINGO

FREE SPACE

@droppinknowledge.com

BINGO

BINGO

BINGO

@droppinknowledge.com

/b/	/k/	/d/	/ee/
/f/	/g/	/ī/	/j/
/l/	/m/	/ō/	/p/
/ar/	/s/	/t/	/ū/
/v/	/z/	/th/	/sh/
/oo/	/ng/	/ch/	/ow/

Answer Key

/b/ - crab
/k/ - duck
/d/ - bird
/e/ - tree
/f/ - giraffe
/g/ - flag
/i/ - fly
/j/ - badge
/k/ - duck
/l/ - snail
/m/ - drum
/n/ - moon
/o/ - piano
/p/ - map
/r/ - star
/s/ - mouse
/t/ - cat
/u/ - menu
/v/ - hive
/z/ - nose
/th/ - tooth
/sh/ - fish
/oo/ - glue
/ng/ - king
/ch/ - bench
/ow/ - cow

BINGO

FREE SPACE

BINGO

BINGO

BINGO

FREE
SPACE

BINGO

BINGO

BINGO

Phonemic Awareness – Ending Sounds

BINGO

BINGO

BINGO

BINGO

Phoneme Addition

BINGO

Say PILL. Now add /ō/ at the end. (pillow)	Say TOP. Now add /s/ to the beginning. (stop)	Say ACHE. Now add /k/ to the beginning. (cake)
Say FOR. Now add /k/ at the end. (fork)	Say LOCK. Now add /k/ to the beginning. (clock)	Say OX. Now add /b/ to the beginning. (box)
Say AND. Now add /h/ to the beginning. (hand)	Say MOO. Now add /n/ to the end. (moon)	Say ROOT. Now add /f/ to the beginning. (fruit)
Say OWN. Now add /f/ to the beginning. (phone)	Say LIP. Now add /k/ to the beginning. (clip)	Say EASE. Now add /ch/ to the beginning. (cheese)

BINGO

Say AIR. Now add /b/ to the beginning. (bear)	Say NAIL. Now add /s/ to the beginning. (snail)	Say ACHE. Now add /r/ to the beginning. (rake)
Say CHESS. Now add /t/ at the end. (chest)	Say ROW. Now add /th/ to the beginning. (throw)	Say PLAY. Now add /n/ to the end. (plane)
Say SAY. Now add /f/ to the end. (safe)	Say PLAN. Now add /t/ to the end. (plant)	Say TRAY. Now add /n/ at the end. (train)
Say LATE. Now add /p/ to the beginning. (plate)	Say SLY. Now add /d/ at the end. (slide)	Say OUCH. Now add /k/ to the beginning. (couch)

BINGO

FREE
SPACE

Phoneme Addition

BINGO

FREE SPACE

@droppinknowledgewithheidi

Phoneme Addition

BINGO

FREE SPACE

@droppinknowledgewithheidi

BINGO

FREE SPACE

@droppinknowledgewithheidi

BINGO

FREE SPACE

Phoneme Addition

BINGO

@droppinknowledgewithheidi

BINGO

FREE
SPACE

BINGO

FREE
SPACE

@droppinknowledgewithheidi

Phoneme Addition

BINGO

Phoneme Addition

BINGO

@droppinknowledgewithheidi

BINGO

FREE SPACE

@droppinknowledgewithheidi

Phoneme Addition

BINGO

hand	moon	plant	cheese	throw
snail	box	clip	rake	cake
couch	clock	**FREE SPACE**	slide	stop
fruit	plane	phone	plate	pillow
safe	bear	chest	train	fork

Phoneme Addition

BINGO

cheese	safe	clock	fruit	snail
box	chest	fork	rake	pillow
clip	slide	**FREE SPACE**	phone	cake
couch	plant	train	throw	moon
stop	hand	plane	bear	plate

BINGO

@droppinknowledgewithheidi

phone	slide	bear	couch	clip
train	plane	plant	plate	fruit
fork	box	**FREE SPACE**	clock	moon
chest	cheese	hand	stop	cake
rake	safe	pillow	throw	snail

Phoneme Addition

BINGO

clip	fruit	hand	cake	snail
throw	fork	safe	moon	plane
phone	train	**FREE SPACE**	couch	bear
plate	pillow	rake	cheese	slide
clock	box	chest	plant	stop

Phoneme Addition

BINGO

throw	fork	plate	chest	box
clip	couch	snail	stop	train
rake	bear	**FREE SPACE**	cheese	hand
cake	fruit	plant	phone	slide
safe	plane	clock	moon	pillow

Phoneme Addition

BINGO

plane	throw	chest	couch	bear
rake	fruit	clip	safe	plant
box	phone	**FREE SPACE**	pillow	stop
moon	fork	clock	train	slide
hand	snail	cheese	cake	plate

Phoneme Addition

BINGO

stop	plant	safe	slide	fruit
cheese	rake	moon	clock	snail
throw	phone	**FREE SPACE**	bear	couch
pillow	train	cake	plane	clip
hand	plate	box	fork	chest

BINGO

chest	box	cheese	safe	throw
clip	pillow	clock	hand	slide
stop	plate	**FREE SPACE**	plant	cake
plane	fork	couch	phone	moon
fruit	rake	train	snail	bear

BINGO

@droppinknowledgewithheidi

throw	plane	slide	cake	bear
couch	fork	stop	hand	chest
pillow	moon	**FREE SPACE**	safe	rake
plant	clock	train	plate	snail
clip	cheese	phone	box	fruit

BINGO

@droppinknowledgewithheidi

moon	chest	fruit	hand	bear
safe	train	clip	cheese	slide
stop	clock	**FREE SPACE**	box	fork
phone	snail	pillow	plant	plane
plate	cake	throw	couch	rake

Phoneme Addition

BINGO

plate	chest	snail	safe	hand
train	moon	bear	clip	phone
rake	pillow	**FREE SPACE**	stop	cake
clock	fork	plant	cheese	plane
box	fruit	slide	couch	throw

Phonemic Awareness – Blending Sounds

BINGO

/ow/ /l/ owl	/h/ /ĕ/ /n/ hen	/y/ /ă/ /k/ yak	/f/ /ĭ/ /sh/ fish
/b/ /ŭ/ /n/ /ē/ bunny	/s/ /l/ /ŏ/ /th/ sloth	/k/ /ă/ /t/ cat	/b/ /ir/ /d/ bird
/d/ /ŏ/ /g/ dog	/b/ /ŭ/ /g/ bug	/f/ /ŏ/ /k/ /s/ fox	/h/ /or/ /s/ horse
/w/ /ā/ /l/ whale	/t/ /ur/ /k/ /ē/ turkey	/d/ /ŭ/ /k/ duck	/s/ /n/ /ā/ /l/ snail
/p/ /ĭ/ /g/ pig	/m/ /oo/ /s/ moose	/sh/ /ar/ /k/ shark	/f/ /r/ /ŏ/ /g/ frog
/m/ /ou/ /s/ mouse	/g/ /ō/ /t/ goat	/s/ /n/ /ā/ /k/ snake	/k/ /r/ /ă/ /b/ crab

BINGO

BINGO

BINGO

FREE SPACE

BINGO

FREE SPACE

BINGO

FREE
SPACE

Phonemic Awareness – Blending Sounds
BINGO

BINGO

Phonemic Awareness – Blending Sounds

BINGO

BINGO

FREE
SPACE

BINGO

BINGO

FREE
SPACE

20 Questions

This is played just like the 20 questions game we all know and love, except students can only ask SOUND questions. For example, I may show my students this image.

20 QUESTIONS

@droppinknowledgewithheidi

PHONEMIC AWARENESS GAME

Then I will think of my word. Now the students may ask yes or no SOUND questions such as:

Does it start with /k/?

Does it end with /t/?

Are there two syllables?

Does it rhyme with bat?

If students ask a non-sound question such as, "Does it end with a G?," I will simply remind them that the question needs to refer to the sounds in the word.

Pro-tip—If you teach younger students, use an image that is less busy. If you teach older students, use a busier image to make it a little more challenging.

We recommend grabbing any image online but you can also use the following link to get a 20 questions digital resource!

https://droppinknowledge.com/droppin-knowledge-on-foundational-skills/

I Spy

This is one of our all-time favorite games because you can use it to work on so many skills! It also requires no prep, as you can spy things around the room. This is a perfect game to play when you have a couple of extra minutes in the day. Here are some ways you can use I Spy:

Phonological Awareness

Syllables: Teacher says, "I spy with my little eye something that has (insert number) syllables!" Students color a picture that contains the correct number of syllables.

Rhyming Words: Have students use the same color to color the pictures that rhyme.

Onset and Rime: Example: I spy a sh-ark and students would color the shark. Onset = the consonant(s) before the first vowel. Rime = trail of letters that follow.

Phonemic Awareness

Beginning Sounds: Teacher says, "I spy with my little eye something that starts with (insert sound)." Students color a picture that starts with that sound. Example: "I spy with my little eye something that starts with /s/" and students could color the sun.

Ending Sounds: Teacher says, "I spy with my little eye something that ends with (insert sound)." Students color a picture that has that ending sound.

Middle Sounds: Teacher says, "I spy with my little eye something that has the (insert sound) in the middle." Students color a picture that has the medial sound.

Blending: Example: "I spy with my little eye a /m/—/u/—/g/." Students would find and color the mug.

PLEASE NOTE: There will usually be more than one option for correct answers!

Do you see the possibilities?

Although you do not need any resources to play this game, sometimes it can be fun to make it a lesson. We have included some I SPY coloring pages for you. There are several ways you can use them.

Whole Group: Print and distribute a coloring page to each student. Call out a word and have students find and color the correct word (please note there may be more than one correct answer).

Centers: Place copies in page protectors. Have students work in pairs. One student is the caller and the other searches for the answer. Students can use expo markers to find answers.

Small Group: For intervention on foundational skills, use the same as you would in whole group practice to reinforce skills in small groups.

I SPY🔍

Words Included for Set 1:

tub	flag
pot	clock
cat	brush
jet	chair
tree	bug
sun	duck
van	fish
web	rake
whale	stick
hat/cap	nail
zip	pen
queen	tie
ham	rat
goat	fan

I SPY

Set 1

Phonemic Awareness Game

@droppinknowledgewithheidi

I SPY

Set 1

Phonemic Awareness Game

I SPY Set 1

Phonemic Awareness Game

@droppinknowledgewithheidi

I SPY

Phonemic Awareness Game

Set 1

@droppinknowledgewithheidi

I SPY

Set 1

Phonemic Awareness Game

@droppinknowledgewithheidi

Words Included for Set 2:

leaf	wheel
shirt	tape
bag	fly
glass	fire
shoe	lamp
truck	six
chain	rug
vase	couch
house	soap
car	screw
sheep	bread/loaf
pig	heart
kite	fork
cone	broom

I SPY

Set 2

Phonemic Awareness Game

@droppinknowledgewithheidi

I SPY

Phonemic Awareness Game

Set 2

I SPY

Set 2

Phonemic Awareness Game

@droppinknowledgewithheidi

I SPY

Set 2

Phonemic Awareness Game

I SPY
Set 2
Phonemic Awareness Game

@droppinknowledgewithheidi

Wrapping Up

Ready, Set, Read On! Your Next Steps and Staying in Touch

We hope you found this book to be an easy, practical read with tools that you can use with your child or your students tomorrow. While we covered a lot, I do want to remind you that this is definitely not an all-inclusive book. Our hope is that this gives you a starting point when working with early or struggling readers.

If you are a teacher like us who was not explicitly taught how to teach kids to read effectively, remember that you do not know better until you do! The good news is that if we follow what the evidence says, 95% of kids *can* learn to read.

Also remember that while much of what is considered the Science of Reading is established, it is still science, and new research is always emerging. We try to attend as many webinars and conferences as we can. We also like to follow the researchers on social media or their websites so we can stay up to date.

We hope you will join Heidi on social media or stay tuned to our website as we continue to share everything we learn and unlearn. Remember, this is a journey! Even well-known researchers and scientists are learning new things all the time.

If you are looking for more support, resources, and training in the Science of Reading check out LitFlix! We have created this space to give you the tools and the training you need to teach reading aligned to the research and evidence. We offer over 10,000 pages of resources (and growing) plus access to several training sessions each month. Learn more at www.scienceofreading101club.com.

Thank you for being open to change and sitting with some uncomfortable feelings as we learn and grow together. Change is not always easy. We often remind ourselves that teaching is not about us, it is about the kids.

We believe that together, we CAN change the literacy statistics!